Piano • Vocal • Guitar

The following songs are the property of:

Bourne Co.
Music Publishers
5 West 37th Street
New York, NY 10018

SOME DAY MY PRINCE WILL COME
WHEN YOU WISH UPON A STAR

ISBN 978-1-4584-1327-7

Walt Disney Music Company
Wonderland Music Company, Inc

Distributed By

7777 W. Bluemound Rd. P.O. Box 13819 Milwaukee, WI 53213

Visit Hal Leonard Online at
www.halleonard.com

CONTENTS

BEAUTY AND THE BEAST

from Walt Disney's BEAUTY AND THE BEAST

Lyrics by HOWARD ASHMAN
Music by ALAN MENKEN

E♭(add9)
E♭
B♭7sus
B♭7
E♭(add9)
E♭
3fr
Just a lit - tle change. Small, to say the
B♭m7
E♭7
A♭maj7
Gm7
Fm7
B♭7sus
B♭7
least. Both a lit - tle scared, nei - ther one pre - pared. Beau - ty and the
poco rit.
E♭(add9)
B♭7sus
Gm
Beast. Ev - er just the same.
a tempo
mf
A♭(add9)
A♭
Gm
A♭(add9)
A♭
4fr
Ev - er a sur - prise. Ev - er as be -

Gm7
Cm
3fr
Cm7
3fr
D♭
E♭
3fr
fore, ev - er just as sure as the sun will rise.
F
C7sus
C7
F(add9)
F
Tale as old as time. Tune as old as
f
C7sus
C7
F(add9)
F
Am
song. Bit - ter - sweet and strange, find - ing you can
B♭(add9)
6fr
B♭
B♭/C
C7
F(add9)
F
C7sus
change, learn - ing you were wrong. Cer - tain as the sun

F(add9) F Cm F7 B♭maj7 Am7

ris - ing in the East. Tale as old as time, song as old as

Gm7 F/C C7 F(add9) F/E Dm Am/C B♭ Am

rhyme. Beau - ty and the Beast. Tale as old as time, song as old as

poco rit. *dim.* *slower*

Gm7 C7sus C7 F(add9) Fsus F(add9)

rhyme. Beau - ty and the Beast.

a tempo

Fsus F

rit.

8va

BELLA NOTTE
(This Is the Night)
from Walt Disney's LADY AND THE TRAMP

Words and Music by PEGGY LEE
and SONNY BURKE

Slowly

B♭

This is the night, it's a beau - ti - ful night, and we

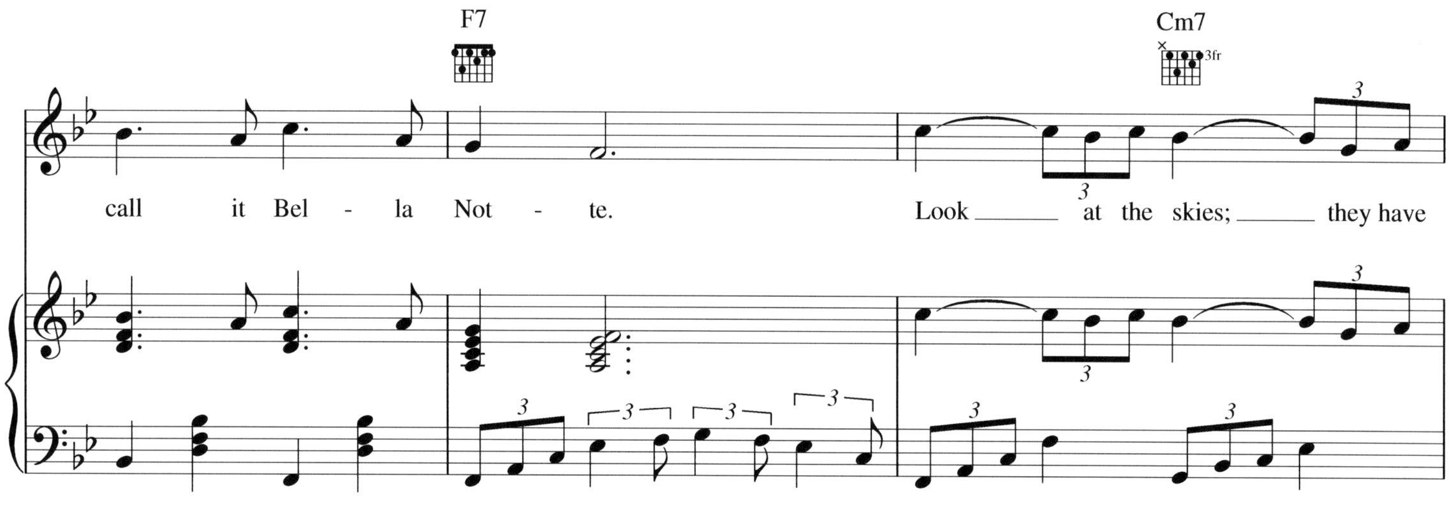

Fm7
Eb♭maj7
B♭+
take this love of your loved one, you'll need it a - bout this
Side by side with your loved one you'll find en - chant - ment
mf
E♭maj7
Gm7
C7
Gm7
time, to keep from fall - ing like a star when you
here. The night will weave its mag - ic spell when the
Cm7
F
F+
B♭
make that diz - zy climb.
one you love is near.
For this is the night and the
Fm
G7
Cm7
F7
F7♭9
B♭
heav-ens are right on this love - ly Bel - la Not - te.

CAN YOU FEEL THE LOVE TONIGHT

from Walt Disney Pictures' THE LION KING

Music by ELTON JOHN
Lyrics by TIM RICE

E♭
B♭/D
E♭
Gm
and it sees me through.
to the wild out - doors
It's e - nough for this rest - less war - rior
when the heart of this star - crossed voy - ag - er
A♭
F
B♭
F/A
just to be with you.
beats in time with yours.
And can you feel the love
poco cresc.
Gm
E♭
B♭
E♭
C/E
to - night?
It is where we are.
F
E♭
B♭/D
It's e - nough for this

Gm
Gm/F
E♭
Cm
B♭/D
E♭
C/E
wide - eyed wan - der - er
that we got this far.
F
B♭
F/A
And can you feel the love
Gm
E♭
B♭
E♭
C/E
to - night,
how it's laid to rest?
F
E♭
B♭/D
It's e - nough to make

Gm
Gm/F
E♭
Cm
B♭/D
E♭
F7sus
kings and vag - a - bonds be - lieve the ver - y best.
E♭/B♭
B♭
poco dim.
1
F/A
E♭/G
B♭/F
E♭
B♭/D
F/A
B♭
Cm7
B♭/D
2
E♭
B♭/D
It's e - nough to make
Gm
Gm/F
E♭
Cm
B♭/D
E♭
F7sus
E♭/B♭
B♭
kings and vag - a - bonds be - lieve the ver - y best.
molto rit.

A DREAM IS A WISH YOUR HEART MAKES

from Walt Disney's CINDERELLA

Words and Music by MACK DAVID,
AL HOFFMAN and JERRY LIVINGSTON

B7
C
when you're fast a - sleep.
E7
Am
D9
4fr
In dreams you will lose your heart - aches;
3
Am7
D7
G
Em7
what - ev - er you wish for you keep.
Am7
D7♯5(♭9)
4fr
G
Have faith in your dreams and some - day
3

Dm7
G7
G7♯5
C
your rain - bow will come smil - ing through.
B
C
F9
G
No mat - ter how your heart is griev - ing, if you keep on be -
A9
Am7
D7
Am7
D9
D7♭9
1
G6
liev - ing, the dream that you wish will come true.
E♭9
D13
2
A♭maj7
G
A true.
8va

IF I NEVER KNEW YOU
(Love Theme from POCAHONTAS)
from Walt Disney's POCAHONTAS

Music by ALAN MENKEN
Lyrics by STEPHEN SCHWARTZ

G
Em
C
if I nev - er felt this love, I would have no ink -
Am7
C
D7sus
- ling of how pre - cious life can be.
G
Em
G
And if I nev - er held you, I would nev - er have
Em7
E7/G♯
Am(add9)
5fr
Cm(maj7)
8fr
Cm6
3fr
a clue how, at last, I'd find in you

Em9
Bm/D
C
Am6(add2)
5fr
the miss - ing part of me.
In this world so
Cmaj7/D
5fr
D9
4fr
Am6(add2)
5fr
Cmaj7/D
5fr
D9
4fr
full of fear,
full of rage and lies,
Bm7
B7/D♯
Em11
5fr
Em7
C
I can see the truth so clear in your eyes, so
D
C/D
G
Em
dry your eyes.
And I'm so grate - ful to you.

G
G/B
C
Am7
G/B
I'd have lived my whole life through, lost for - ev - er
C
C/D
C
D/C
C
D/C
C
3
if I nev - er knew you.
E♭maj7(no3rd)
F
B♭
Gm
3fr
Female: If I nev - er knew you,
B♭
Gm
3fr
E♭
3fr
I'd be safe but half as real, nev - er know - ing I

B♭/C
Cm
E♭
F7sus
could feel a love so strong and true.
B♭
Gm
B♭
I'm so grate - ful to you. I'd have lived my whole
B♭/D
E♭
Cm7
B♭/D
E♭
E♭/F
life through, lost for - ev - er if I nev - er knew
F/E♭
E♭maj7
F/E♭
E♭
F/E♭
Male: I thought our love would be so beau - ti - ful.
you.

Dm7
F/G
Gm7
F/G
Female:
Some - how we'd make the whole world bright.
Both: I nev - er knew that fear and
E♭maj7
B♭/D
Gm
Dm7
E♭
hate could be so strong, all they'd leave us were these whis - pers in the night,
but
Cm9
Dm7
E♭
E♭/F
F/G
still my heart is say - ing we were right.
Female: Oh.
C
Am
C
Male: There's no mo - ment I re - gret
If I nev - er knew you, if I nev - er knew

Am
F
C/D
Dm
since the mo - ment that we met. If our time has
this love, I would have no ink - ling of how
F
F/G
G
F/G
Em/G
F/G
gone too fast I've lived at last.
pre - cious life can be.
G
F/G
Em/G
G/F
Fmaj7
G/F
F
Both: I thought our love would be so
beau - ti - ful,
Em7
some - how we'd make the whole world

G/F
Fmaj7
G/F
F
bright.
Female: I thought our love would be so
Em7
G/A
3fr
C/G
beau - ti - ful,
we'd turn the dark - ness in - to light.
Both: And
Dm7
Em7
F
E♭m7/A♭
6fr
still my heart is say - ing we were right.
Male: We were right. And
D♭
B♭m
D♭
Female: If I nev - er knew you,
if I nev - er knew you,
I'd have lived my

Fm7
Gbmaj7
Ebm7
6fr
Fm7
Gb(add9)
whole life through Female: emp - ty as the sky,
Ebm7
6fr
Fm7
Gbmaj7
Freely
Bbm7
Db/F
Both: nev - er know - ing why,
lost for - ev - er
rit.
Gb
Ab7sus
4fr
Ab7
4fr
Db
Bbm
if I nev - er knew you.
a tempo
Gb
Ab7
4fr
Db(add9)
rit.

ENDLESS NIGHT

from Disney Presents THE LION KING: THE BROADWAY MUSICAL

Music by LEBO M, HANS ZIMMER
and JAY RIFKIN
Lyrics by JULIE TAYMOR

D
Em/D
D
D/C♯
Bm
D/A
G
Home is an emp - ty dream, lost to the
D/F♯
D
Em
D/F♯
night.
Fa - ther, I feel so a -
Steadily
A
Em
lone.
You prom - ised you'd be there
mf
D
A/C♯
when-ev - er I need - ed you.
When-ev - er I call your name,

A
Em
you're not an - y - where.
I'm try - ing to hold on,
D
A/C♯
To Coda
just wait - ing to hear your voice.
One word, just a word will do
A
D
Em/D
to end this night - mare.
When will the
mp rall.
a tempo
D
D/C♯
Bm
D/A
G
D/F♯
dawn - ing break,
oh,
end - less
night?

D
Em7
D/F#
Em7
D
A
Sleep - less, I dream of the day
D
Em/D
D
D/C#
Bm
D/A
G
when you were by my side, guid - ing my
mf
D/F#
D
Em7
D/F#
Em7
D
path.
Fa - ther, I can't find the
A
D.S. al Coda
way.
CODA
A
to end this night - mare.
mp

D
G/D
F♯m/D
D
I know that this night must end
and that the sun will rise,
p
G/D
F♯m/D
D
and that the sun will rise.
I know that the clouds must clear
G/D
F♯m/D
D
G/D
F♯m/D
D
and that the sun will shine,
and that the sun will shine.
G
A6
Bm7
I know that this night will end
and that the sun will rise,
cresc. poco a poco

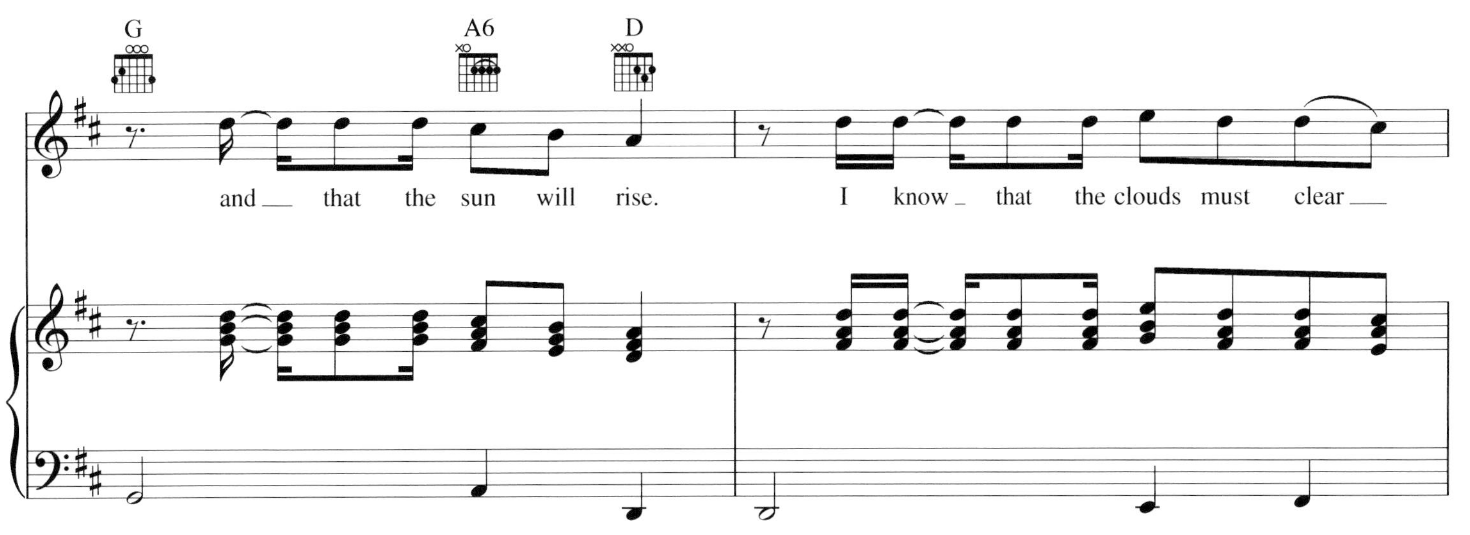
G
A6
D
and that the sun will rise.
I know that the clouds must clear

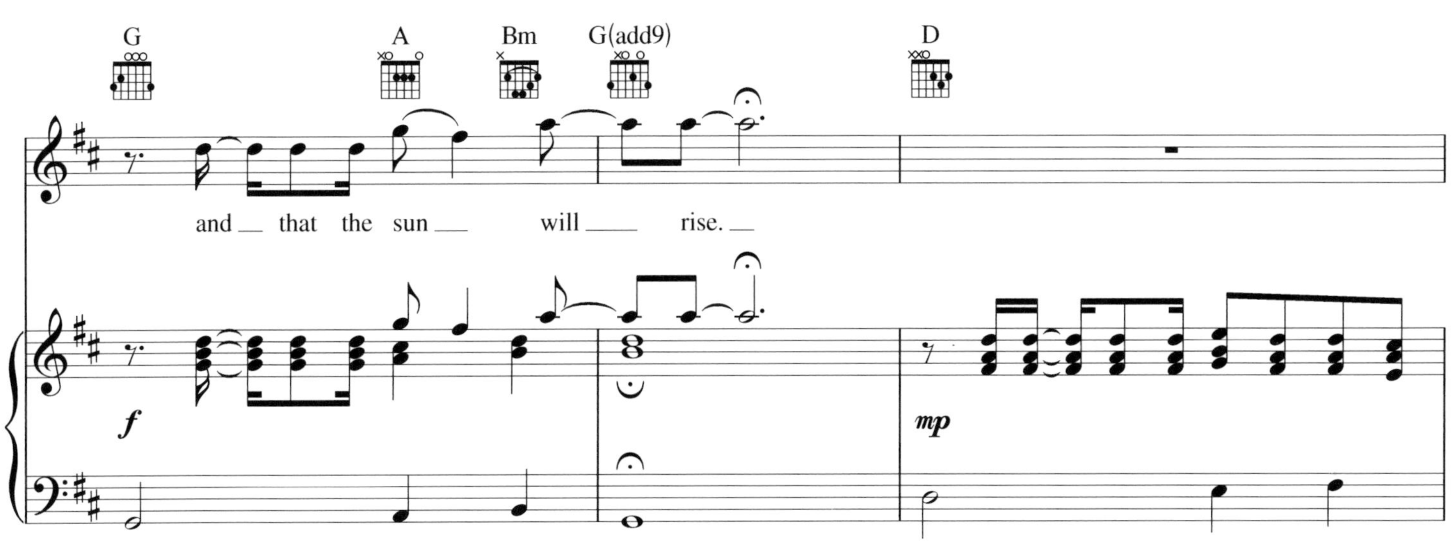
G
A
Bm
G(add9)
D
and that the sun will rise.
f
mp

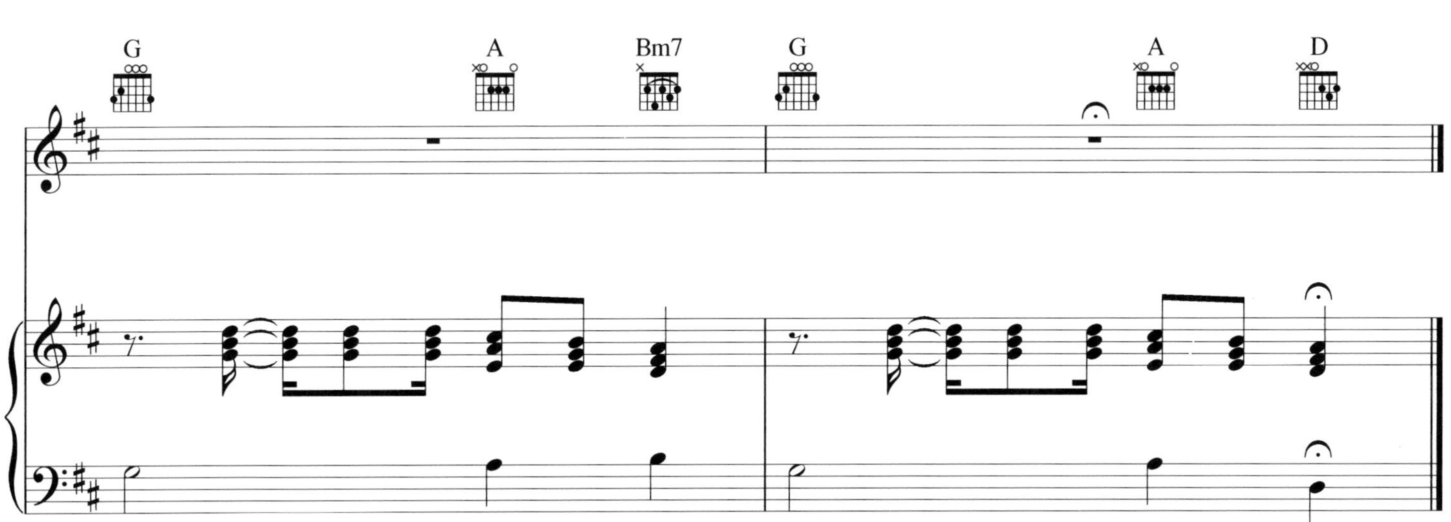
G
A
Bm7
G
A
D

LAVENDER BLUE
(Dilly Dilly)
from Walt Disney's SO DEAR TO MY HEART

Words by LARRY MOREY
Music by ELIOT DANIEL

C
F
C/G
F/A
D7
so? I told my - self, dil - ly, dil - ly,
Dm7/G
G7
C
F
I told me so. If your dil - ly, dil - ly heart feels a
Em7
A9
5fr
Em7
A7
dil - ly, dil - ly way and if you'll an - swer "yes," in a
G/D
D7
pret - ty lit - tle church on a dil - ly, dil - ly day
you'll
I'll
be wed in a

G7 C G Gm7 C9

dil - ly, dil - ly dress of lav - en - der blue, dil - ly, dil - ly,

F C F

lav - en - der green; then {I'll / you'll} be

C/G F/A Dm7 G7

king, dil - ly, dil - ly, and {you'll / I'll} be {my / your}

1 C C/E F D7/F♯ Dm7/G G7 | 2 C F/C Csus C

queen. ___ | queen. ___

SOMETHING THERE

from Walt Disney's BEAUTY AND THE BEAST

Lyrics by HOWARD ASHMAN
Music by ALAN MENKEN

1
D(add9)
A7sus
A7
D(add9)
fore?
p
A7sus
A7
F(add9)
C7sus
C7
A7sus
A7
N.C.
2
D
Beast: She glanced this
fore.
cresc.
mf
With pedal
G
D/F#
Em7
G/A
3fr
Belle: New, and a bit a -

F♯m
B7sus
2fr
B7
Bm7
E7
larm - ing.
Who'd have ev - er thought that
Em/A
A9
5fr
C/D
D
C/D
D
C/E
D
this could be?
cresc.
G
Gmaj7
G6
G
F♯m
True that he's no Prince Charm - ing,
f
B7sus
2fr
B7
Esus
but there's some - thing in him that I

E7
A
Em/A
A
N.C.
sim - ply did - n't see.
Lumiere: Well, who'd have
dim.
mp
A7sus/D
A7/C♯
D
Mrs. Potts: Well, bless my soul!
Well, who in - deed?
thought?
Cogsworth: Well, who'd have known?
Lumiere: And who'd have
A7sus/D
A7/C♯
D
D7/C
It's so pe - cu - liar!
guessed they'd come to - geth - er on their own?
All 3: Wait and
G/B
Gm/B♭
F♯7/A♯
B7/A
see... a few days more.
There may be

Em/G
A7
D(add9)
D
N.C.
some-thing there that was-n't there be - fore.
Cogsworth: Per-haps there's
A7sus
A7
Dsus
D
N.C.
some-thing there that was-n't there be - fore!
Mrs. Potts: There may be
A7sus
A7
D(add9)
some - thing there that was - n't there be - fore.
Chip: What's there, Mama?
Mrs. Potts: Ssh. I'll tell you when you're older. Come along, Chip. Let's give them some privacy.
rit.

LOVE IS A SONG

from Walt Disney's BAMBI

Words by LARRY MOREY
Music by FRANK CHURCHILL

C7
Gm
3fr
F
C7/G
F
ing.
Hope
may
die,
yet
love's
ing.
Like
the
voice
of
a
mf
Gm
3fr
C7
F
A7
Dm
Dm7
beau - ti - ful
mu - sic
comes
each
heav - en - ly
choir,
love's
sweet
1
G7
Gm
3fr
C7
day
like
the
dawn.
rit.
2
Gm7
C7
F
mu - sic
flows
on.

PART OF YOUR WORLD

from Walt Disney's THE LITTLE MERMAID

Music by ALAN MENKEN
Lyrics by HOWARD ASHMAN

Bb
C/Bb
Bb
Look at this trove, treas-ures un-told. How man-y won-ders can
C/Bb
Am7
Dm7
one cav-ern hold? Look-ing a-round here you'd think, sure, she's got
F/G
G7
Bbmaj7
ev-'ry-thing. I've got gad-gets and giz-mos a-
Am7
F/A
Dm7
F/G
G7
plen-ty. I've got who-zits and what-zits ga-lore. You want

B♭maj7
Am7
F/A
Dm7
thing - a - ma bobs, I've got twen - ty. But who cares? No big
rall.
F/G
G7
B♭/C
Am/C
B♭/C
C7
deal. I want more.
a tempo
F
Am7
B♭
I wan - na be where the peo - ple are. I wan - na see wan - na
a tempo
B♭/C
C
Dm
Am
see 'em danc - in', walk - in' a - round on those, what - d' - ya call 'em, oh,

B♭/C
C
C7
F
feet.
Flip - pin' your fins ___ you don't
F/A
B♭
B♭/C
C
get too far. ___
Legs are re - quired ___ for jump - in', danc - in'.
Dm
Am
F/A
B♭/C
Stroll - in' a - long ___ down the, what's that word a - gain, street?
C7
F
F/E♭
Up where they walk, up where they run, up where they

B♭/D
B♭m/D♭
F/C
stay all day in the sun.
Wan - der - in' free, wish I could
B♭/C
C
F
be part of that world.
What would I
B♭
C/B♭
Am
give if I could live out - ta these wa - ters?
Dm
B♭
C/B♭
What would I pay to spend a day warm on the

Am
F7sus
F7
B♭
sand? Bet - cha on land they un - der -
C/B♭
A7sus
A7
Dm
Dm/C
stand. Bet they don't re - pri - mand their daugh - ters. Bright young
F/G
G
F/G
G
E♭maj7
3fr
wom - en, sick of swim - min' read - y to stand.
rall.
a tempo
B♭/C
C
B♭/C
C
F
F/A
And read - y to know what the peo - ple know.

B♭maj7
B♭/C
Ask 'em my ques - tions and get some an - swers.
Dm
Am
F/A
What's a fire, and why does it, what's the word,
Gm7
C7
F
burn? When's it my turn? Would - n't I
F/E♭
B♭/D
B♭m/D♭
love, love to ex - plore that shore up a - bove,

F
out of the sea.
Wish I could
slower
B♭/C
C7
B♭
be
part of that world.
L.H.
C/B♭
B♭
C/B♭
F

SO THIS IS LOVE
(The Cinderella Waltz)
from Walt Disney's CINDERELLA

Words and Music by MACK DAVID,
AL HOFFMAN and JERRY LIVINGSTON

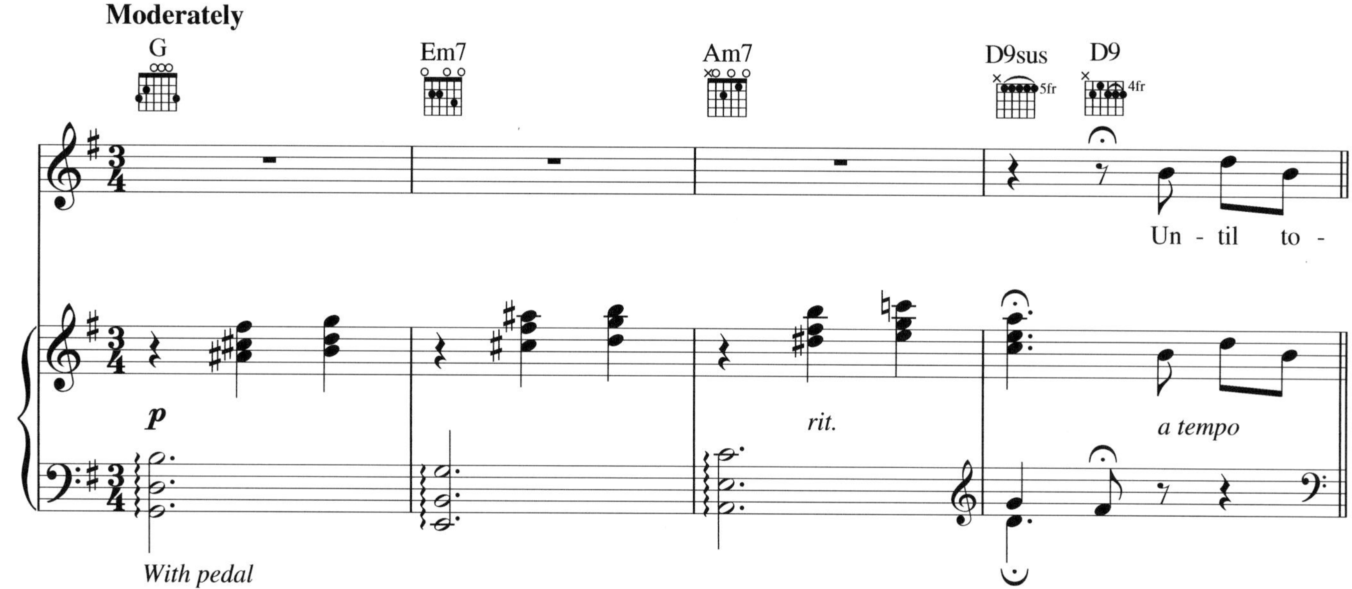

Em7
A7
D9
4fr
But now it's as clear as can be.
G
G♯dim
6fr
So this is love, mm so this is
Am7
D9
4fr
G
Gmaj9♯5
G6
Bm7
2fr
love, so this is what makes life di-
Am7
D9
4fr
D7
vine. I'm all a - glow, mm

B♭dim
D7
and now I know the
Am7
D13
F9♭5
E9
E♭9
D9
key to all hea - ven is mine. My heart has
G
G♯dim
Am7
wings, mm and I can fly.
D9
G
G7
Dm7
G7
C
I'll touch ev - 'ry star in the sky.

Am7
D7
Am7
Am9
D9
4fr
So this is the mir - a - cle that
G
Bm7
2fr
E7
Am7
I've been dream - ing of, so this is love, mm
D9
4fr
Am7
D7♭9
4fr
1
G
E♭9
D9
4fr
so this is love. So this is
2
G
Em7
Am7
G
love.

SOME DAY MY PRINCE WILL COME

from Walt Disney's SNOW WHITE AND THE SEVEN DWARFS

Words by LARRY MOREY
Music by FRANK CHURCHILL

Gm7 C7 F A+ B♭dim
me. He'll whis - per, "I love
beat. Some day we'll say and
D7 Gm B♭+/F♯ C7
you" and steal a kiss or two. Though he's
do things we've been long - ing to. Though she's
F A7 A+ B♭+ Bdim F Adim
far a - way I'll find my love some day, some day when my
Gm7 C7 1 F A♭7 Gm7 C7 2 F
dreams come true. true.
3fr
4fr
8vb

A WHOLE NEW WORLD

from Walt Disney's ALADDIN

Music by ALAN MENKEN
Lyrics by TIM RICE

D
I can o - pen your eyes, take you won - der by
G/B A/C♯ Em/G F♯7 F♯7/A♯ Bm Bm/A
4fr
won - der, o - ver, side - ways and un - der on a
G D A
mag - ic car - pet ride. A whole new world,
D A A7/C♯ D(add9) D
a new fan - tas - tic point of view. No one to
3

A/G
D/F♯
A/G
D/F♯
Bm7
E7sus
E7
tell us no or where to go or say we're on - ly dream -
G/A
3fr
A
D
ing. A whole new world, a daz - zling
A
A♯dim7
Bm
D7/A
A/G
D/F♯
place I nev - er knew. But when I'm way up here, it's
3
A/G
D/F♯
Bm7
E7sus
E7
C
A7sus
A7
crys - tal clear that now I'm in a whole new world with

D
F
you.
Un - be - liev - a - ble
sights,
in - de - scrib - a - ble
B♭/D
C/E
feel - ing.
Gm/B♭
A7sus
A7/C♯
Dm
Dm/C
B♭
Soar - ing, tum - bling, free - wheel - ing through an end - less dia - mond sky.
F
C
F
A whole new world,
a hun - dred

C F C/B♭ F/A

thou - sand things be - gin. I'm like a shoot - ing star, I've

C/B♭ F/A Dm7 G7sus G7 B♭/C

come so far; I can't go back. I'm in a whole new

C F C C♯dim7

world ___ with new ho - ri - zons to ___ pur - sue. ___

Dm F7/C C/B♭ F/A C/B♭ F/A

___ I'll chase them an - y - where. There's time to spare.

Dm7
G7sus
G7
E♭
3fr
B♭/C
C7
Dm
Let me share this whole new world with you.
F/C
B♭(add9)
6fr
F/A
Gm7(add4)
A whole new world, that's where we'll be.
F/A
B♭(add9)
6fr
C7sus
F
A thrill - ing chase, a won - drous place for you and me.
rit.

WHEN YOU WISH UPON A STAR

from Walt Disney's PINOCCHIO

Cdim C C6/G C/E E♭dim7 Dm Am/E F F/G G9 G7♭9
3fr
9fr
who you are, an - y - thing your heart de - sires will come to
Cmaj7 G13 G7 C A7 Dm Dm7 G7
3fr
you. If your heart is in your dream, no re - quest is
Cdim C C6/G C/E E♭dim7 Dm Am/E F F/G G9
3fr
9fr
too ex - treme, when you wish up - on a star as dream - ers
C Fm6/G Em/G Cmaj7 C6 Dm/G Gdim G7
do. Fate is kind, she brings to

Cdim
C
Am
D7
those who love, the sweet ful - fill - ment of their se - cret
Fm6
G7
G7♯5(♭9)
G7
C
A7
Dm
Dm7
long - ing. Like a bolt out of the blue,
G7
Cdim
C
C6/G
C/E
E♭dim7
Dm
Am/E
F
fate steps in and sees you thru, when you wish up - on a star your
1
F/G
G9
G7♭9
C
G13
G7
2
F/G
G7
C
dream comes true. dream comes true.